The Wit and Wisdom Mother

WISE ADVCE FOR ANY AGE

Ceezar Martinson

Dedication

This book is dedicated to my mother who remains the most fascinating person I know.

CHAPTER 1

Stupidity

The first quote came from a conversation with my mother when I was 13 about trying to understand the failures of lack of intellectual thought. The second quote stems from a conversation where my mother described the harm that stupid people can cause when they have decision-making authority. The last quote is the definition my mother has always given when asked how she defines stupidity.

Stupidity is both a failure of common sense and a failure to engage in critical thinking.

When you let a group of idiots form a committee with decision-making power, you have convened a force of destruction more dangerous than a hydrogen bomb.

Ignorance is, I don't know. Stupidity is that I don't know and don't want to know.

Love

These quotes come from conversations over the years about the nature of love. My mother said everything about her experience of being married to my father for over 53 years.

Love is about realizing what you need in life to survive emotionally.

If you genuinely love someone, you are ready, willing and able to compromise. Love is not a dictatorship but a partnership between two people.

Sacrifice is foundational to love. Without it, you would not have a loving relationship.

CHAPTER 3

Courage

The first quote was from a conversation with my mother about moments in her life when she had been threatened with life-threatening danger and how she showed courage. The second quote describes her observations of courageous people in her life. The last quote was from our conversation about how Aristotle described courage and why it lacks virtues.

Courage is not the absence of fear. It is feeling fear and choosing not to let fear overwhelm you from doing what must be done.

A courageous person does not seek approval from others. They set off on their journey with the intent to help another regardless of the consequences to themselves.

Courage is a virtue. However, of the virtues, it is most profoundly lacking in most people. When you encounter courageous people, you need to hold them close because they are rare.

CHAPTER 4

Patience

The first quote comes from a conversation my mother and I had about a project I was working on in high school and how I needed to take my time on it. The final quote came about from my mother sharing a painful story from her childhood and what the experience taught her.

Nothing in life of any value happens without patience.

Patience is not innate to us as human beings. It is a learned behavior.

To gain a great deal of patience in life, one must go through difficult moments, for it is in the genuinely stressful and challenging moments that we learn the most significant amount of patience.

CHAPTER 5

Wisdom

These quotes concerning wisdom were all made by my mother when describing different life experiences she has had. They all fit into a category of lessons learned for her.

To attain wisdom in your life, you have to experience failure. If there is no failure in your life, there is no wisdom.

One way to seek wisdom in your life is through reading great books. Another way is to seek wise people with lived experiences who can give you a practical tutorial.

Wisdom can always be found no matter how ridiculous or stupid a situation is. The question is whether you are actively seeking it.

CHAPTER 6

Marriage

As someone who has been married for over 50 years, I believe all of these quotes come from lived experience in a loving, stable relationship.

Any romantic relationship that is genuinely worth something leads to marriage.

Marriage is not supposed to be emotionally or physically abusive. The purpose of marriage is to uplift both men and women.

Constant and honest communication is the essence of a good marriage. If you cannot speak honestly to the other person or consistently to the other person, there is no possibility of a good marriage.

CHAPTER 7

Peace

My mother firmly believes that peace on Earth is a fantasy people have that will never happen. However, she has spoken of the idea over the years in different circumstances, and the quotes reflect that.

Peace on Earth is a dream that men have had for centuries. It will never happen because human nature has a strong current of violence within it.
To advocate for others to be peaceful, you must first make yourself calm.

Pursuing peace does not mean that you abandon violence, for in cases where your life is threatened or the lives of those you love, violence to prevent the loss of life is the only moral course of action.

CHAPTER 8

Natural Resources

She has always supported natural resource development and the good it can provide communities. She has also been concerned with how those resources are managed for the public benefit, and the quotes deal with those concerns.

There is an abundance of natural resources on this planet to generate much-needed wealth and prosperity for the people of this world. There needs to be more honest politicians who priorities the well-being of the people as opposed to a select group of corrupt interests.

With natural resource development, modern science as we know it and our entire civilization would exist.

When considering the development of natural resources, we must consider our long-term goals, not just the short-term benefits we are getting now.

CHAPTER 9

Advice

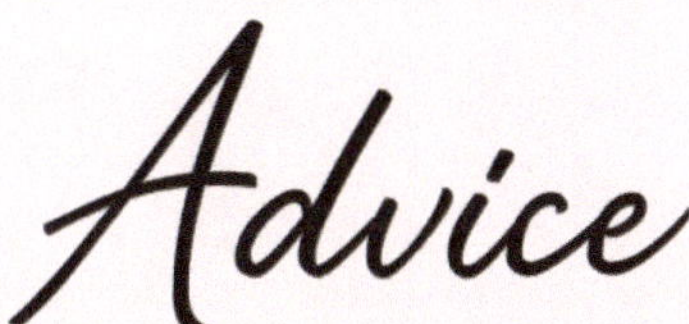

She has always believed in listening to advice offered by others and, where possible, taking good advice and using it to one's advantage.

Wise men don't need it, and fools don't need it.

To give someone good advice, you have to get to know the person. Otherwise, you could be leading them in a direction that may harm them instead of helping them.

One of the significant aspects of giving advice is life experience. If you have not gone through any seriously tough moments, you cannot advise people on facing adverse to-face

CHAPTER 10

Travel

Mom has been all over the world. So, travel has a special meaning to her, and this is a topic she has spoken about many times over the years.

To truly value your trips, you have to make those trips rare. When travel becomes familiar, it destroys the value of seeing new places.

The most essential part of any traveling you do is making sure you have the right person with you. And by that, I mean someone who is not a moron who will spend the trip causing you problems.

Before taking a trip, do preliminary research on where you are going. It will help enhance the experience when you get there.

CHAPTER 11

Parenting

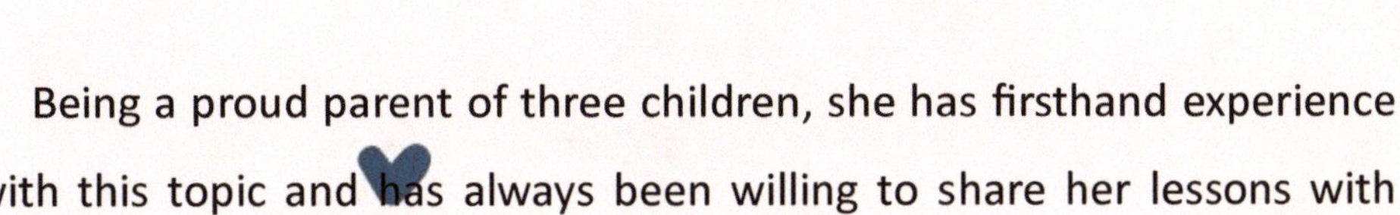

Being a proud parent of three children, she has firsthand experience with this topic and has always been willing to share her lessons with others.

Being a parent is not about being liked by your children. If you want to win a popularity contest, you have no business raising children.

One of the most foundational aspects of parenting is establishing discipline with your children. When you discipline your child, you do so from a place of love. When the world disciplines your child, it will not be from a place of love.

When raising children, you must be careful of the adults you expose them to. The wrong adults in a child's life can spell disaster when that child reaches maturity.

CHAPTER 12

Desire

Due to dealing with friends who have struggled with drug addiction, this is a subject that she dealt with all too often.

Desire is not by itself an evil. However, unchecked desire can cause tremendous harm to oneself and others.

To attempt to live some semblance of a moral life, it is genuinely critical to examine one's desires. If you never question your desires, you are not a person of character.

One of the most fascinating aspects of the human condition is how people place their desires at the forefront of their lives as though their desires are a deity.

The Study of History

Mom has always loved history; as a young child, she always gave me biographies to read about different historical figures. These quotes reflect that passion.

History doesn't repeat itself because every period is unique unto itself. But there are themes that you see in history. One prominent example is the battle between freedom and tyranny that has played out across many societies.

History is one of the most critical fields in the humanities, and yet it is disregarded by so many. The consequences of that disregard can be seen in our leadership failure at many societal levels.

Most people don't take the time to study and understand their history, so how can they be expected to research and learn the history of entire civilizations?

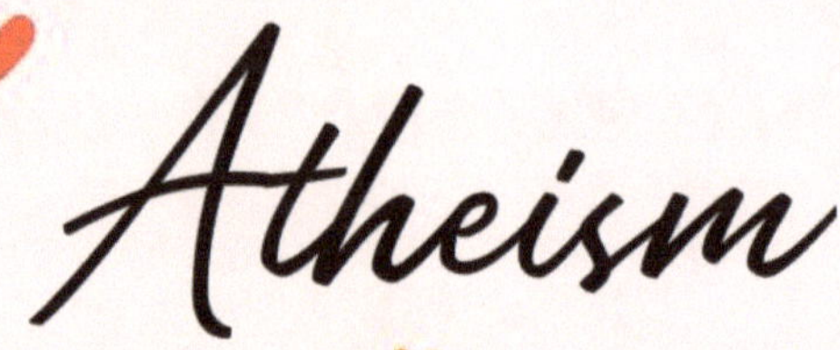

CHAPTER 14

Atheism

Mom has always been a devout Christian and has never had a high regard for atheism as a philosophical system. The quotes reflect that.

The notion that our existence is meaningless is one of the most stupid and morally debased ideas ever put forward in Western philosophy.

I have found it interesting when atheists claim that the only things that are fundamental in this world are those things that can be proven by the scientific method. Love, for example, is genuine, and all people experience it, yet it cannot be proven via the scientific method.

The notion of transcendence is the very basis of our humanity. No one explains how a system works from within the system. The God's eye description is always used to show how fundamental it is to our humanity.

CHAPTER 15

Adoption

Mom has witnessed people taking it upon themselves to adopt a child and has permanently been moved by the selflessness of the gesture. These quotes are from some very moving conversations on the subject.

Adopting a child is one of the most selfless acts of love one can bestow on another.

When you adopt a child, you are taking a leap of faith that is so very rare in a world where we are constantly told to have faith in nothing.

I like to think of Adoption as taking the future of another person into your hands and giving that person endless possibilities.

CHAPTER 16

Desire

She has always been and always will love the writing of Stephen King.

His work is so profound that he understands that evil is a supernatural force that influences human affairs.

The character development in his books is the best I have seen from an author in 30 years. If you are going to write, give me characters with depth.

His best novel is The Stand. It is his best because he brought a Lord of the Rings-style adventure to the horror genre, which is a magnificent feat.

CHAPTER 17

Agatha Christie

She has read more short story collections from this author than she imagined. I grew up with her reading me Christie novels to get me to sleep at night.

What made her a great crime writer was her understanding of human nature.

Hercule Poirot was a great detective because he followed the truth no matter where it lead.

Hercule Poirot was my favorite detective by Christie. But I don't know that I have a favorite novel because each story was unique, and the explored themes were of great value to themselves.

CHAPTER 18

Writing

Most of the writing Mom has done over the years has been technical. She has always enjoyed a good novel and has spoken often of what it takes to be a great writer.

To write well, one must be an avid reader. Reading gives one the vocabulary to write.

The best way to get into the habit of writing is to start by doing a lot of technical writing because it gets you into the habit of writing. From there, one can go on to writing fiction.

Writing as a skill set is extremely valuable because it allows you to expand your horizons and communicate with people you would never meet in your ordinary life.

CHAPTER 19

Mental Illness

As someone who has witnessed family members and friends struggle with mental illness, the subject of insanity was just regular kitchen table talk growing up.

Insanity does not happen overnight. It takes place over time; the signs are there if you pay attention.

The human mind is like a beehive. Many chambers connect, and when one is damaged, it causes cracks in all the others.

Refusing to accept reality is only one part of madness. The other part is attempting to get other people to join in.

CHAPTER 20

God

As someone who has indeed been through some difficult and, without question, life-threatening situations, the subject of God is enormous in my mother's life.

In my many wanderings of life, I have concluded that God is a teacher and that the world is his classroom. The question is, how much have we learned in the course of our lives before we get to him?

One of the most profound insights into the nature of God can be found in the Bible is the dialogue that takes place between God and Abraham. It is an intellectual dialogue showing that He can be reasoned with as a being.

CHAPTER 21

Judaism

Some very close friends of hers are Orthodox Jews as well as Holocaust survivors, and she has appreciated all they have shared about their Jewish faith.

Without the history presented in the Old Testament, it would have been impossible to grasp the significance of the Gospel.

The Ten Commandments is a set of moral laws that profoundly changed the entire course of civilization itself. Every person everywhere should be profoundly grateful to the Jewish people for sharing the commandments with humanity.

CHAPTER 22

Anti-Semitism

About 25 years ago, Mom went to Warsaw, Poland. Before she left, she took a tour of Auschwitz, and it was a tour that forever changed her life.

Anti-Semitism is an ancient evil. It will never be eradicated; it is up to each new generation to continue the fight against it.

Anti-Semites have never changed their arguments or even the tactics they use to advance their detestable agenda. What does change is how open a society is to its age-old deceptions.

CHAPTER 23

Winston Churchill

She has spent her entire life reading biographies of Churchill and has always found inspiration in his life and leadership during World War II.

He set out to study as much as he could of the world around him and, in so doing, became an amazing polymath.

To understand how Churchill became the most outstanding leader of the 20th century, you have to look at the wars he had previously fought. From those successes and failures, he learned how to defeat the greatest enemy of his life, Adolf Hitler.

What makes Churchill's life so profound is not merely the fact that he saved the world but that he was a prophetic figure. He saw the great horrors of the 20th century coming and planned accordingly.

CHAPTER 24

Immortality

Mom has been fascinated by immortality for years, owing to her general interest in science fiction and philosophy.

In examining the concept of immortality, I think Star Trek got it right. You would be bored as hell.

I would not want to live forever because human nature will not change no matter what century or technological advancement comes along.

The chief question about immortal existence is whether you will be eternal by yourself or with others. Immortality would be impossible for one person alone, but if it is within a group context, you can make it through centuries in a mentally stable way.

CHAPTER 25

Satan

35 years ago, my mother participated in an exorcism, and the experience has haunted her to this very day. These quotes reflect her private meditations on the Devil and his role in human affairs.

The Devil, in contrast to God, is a dictator who demands total obedience from his followers. It is this among many reasons why he should not be worshiped.

When Christ faced the Devil in the desert, the Devil proved that he was a master at deception. And Christ showed us that to defeat him, we must learn to think critically to counter his lies.

There are satanic cults all around us. The most dangerous thing about them is that they are made up of ordinary people to better pull us into that darkness.

CHAPTER 26

Science

As a science fiction nerd, my mother has always been fascinated by science and the process of technological development. However, she has also always been concerned about the ethics behind science, and these quotes reflect that.

Science explains how life and our broader universe work. But science does not give us any answers on why it works.

Science without a moral foundation becomes a dystopian nightmare humanity struggles to escape.

One of the most profound inventions in the history of science has been the development of nuclear power. It is a technology that can send us into the very depths of space for the colonization of entire planets, or it can lead to the destruction of our own.

CHAPTER 27

Ethics

These quotes are based on conversations my mother and I have had over the years on ethics and why studying and understanding right and wrong is essential.

Ethics is one of the most important fields of philosophy because humankind must understand right from wrong for our species to maintain any semblance of civilization.

People often speak of the importance of ethics, but when it comes down to the wire, they abandon ethical considerations very quickly. This is because courage is vital to ethics; it is not enough to know what is right. You have to choose it.

The place where the teaching of ethics begins is in the home. If parents do not instill some moral compass in their children, then no one else can shape that child into a model citizen.

Martin Luther King Jr.

My mother, as a teenager in the Jim Crow South, participated in the Civil Rights Movement. These quotes reflect her views on Dr. King and the leadership he provided at a critical time in American history.

He was a prophet, so he knew he would die. That is why his sermons are so profound and resonate many years after his death.

He spoke against segregation not from the position of the suffering of black Americans but as a Christian pastor calling us as a nation to heed God's law and respect the fundamental dignity of our fellow man.

In examining the movement he led, it can be stated without any reservation that had he not been leading the civil rights cause, it would not have achieved the victories it did.

CHAPTER 29

Black Nationalism

My mother was active as a teenager in the civil rights movement of the 1960s in the Jim Crow South. These quotes reflect her outlook on Black Nationalism and why she rejects that philosophy.

Our goal as black people should not be to oppress whites or any other people but to live in freedom and harmony with others. Adopting our tribalistic mentality will be our doom.

Black Nationalism and Neo-Nazism are just two sides of the same coin. The only difference is whom they wish to impose tyranny on.

As a black woman, I wish to live in a society where people see me for the depth of character that I have and not examine my race.

CHAPTER 30

Leadership

The first quote concerns how my mother has always defined the difference between being a boss and a leader. The second quote concerns a quality of leadership my mother has always felt needs to be present for someone to be defined as a leader. The last quote is how my mother has always judged people in leadership who are truly good at what they do.

A leader says follow me. A boss says to do that.

Leadership is about inspiration. If you cannot inspire people, then you cannot lead them.

Leadership is not about taking credit for the success that comes along. It is about taking responsibility for the failures and allowing your team to regroup.

About the Author

Cezar Martinson is a lifelong Alaskan who got his start writing professionally at the Anchorage Press writing about the Alaska Legislature and the state budget process. Apart from writing he enjoys reading, bike riding, and camping in the great Alaska wilderness.